# INTERIOR SPACES

## OF THE USA AND CANADA

### VOLUME 5

A PICTORIAL REVIEW

# INTERIOR SPACES

## OF THE USA AND CANADA

**VOLUME 5**

A PICTORIAL REVIEW

ISBN 1 86470 030 0
© 2000
The Images Publishing Group Pty Ltd
Melbourne, Australia 2000
Printed by Leefung–Asco Printers

# Contents

# Commercial Space and Atria

1

3

2

4

5

6

**Volan Design Office Interior**
**Boulder, Colorado**
Abo•Copeland Architecture, Inc.

1   Entrance and reception area introduce 'high design' image
2   'Arcade' circulation corridor unifies generous interior volume
3   Private office interior
4   Conference room
5   Conference room from 'commons'
6   'Commons' environment enhances working in teams
Photo credit: Abo • Copeland Architecture, Inc.

1

2

3

**415 Central Park West Lobby
New York, New York**
Alfredo De Vido Architects

1&2　Renovation of lobby in pre-war
　　　apartment building
Photo credit: courtesy Alfredo De Vido Architects

**Council Chamber, Fresno City Hall,
Fresno, California**
Arthur Erickson Architects with Lew/
Patnaude and Edward S. Darden, Fresno

3　Council Chamber from a rear balcony for
　　the public
Photo credit: courtesy Arthur Erickson Architects

**RealNames Corporation Offices
San Carlos, California**
Blauel Architects

4　Non-hierarchial working along service
　　spines
5　Floor layout with core and fully glazed
　　envelope
6　Espresso bar with 'chill-out' area
Photo credit: VIEW/Dennis Gilbert

4

5

1

2

3

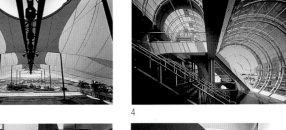

4

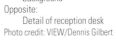

5

**RealNames Corporation Offices**
**San Carlos, California**
Blauel Architects
Previous pages:
    Reception with meeting rooms in
    background
Opposite:
    Detail of reception desk
Photo credit: VIEW/Dennis Gilbert

**Courtyard of the Canadian Chancery**
**Washington, DC**
Arthur Erickson Architects
  1  Exterior
  2  Foyer, looking out toward entrance
Photo credit: courtesy Arthur Erickson Architects

**San Diego Convention Centre**
**San Diego, California**
Arthur Erickson Architects with Deems Lewis
McKinley & Loschky Marquardt & Nesholm
  3  View of canopy covered roof, exhibition
     and event area
  4  Mezzanine under barrel vaulted foyer
  5  Upper mezzanine level
Photo credit: courtesy Arthur Erickson Architects

**WebGensis**
**New York, New York**
Alfredo De Vido Architects
  6  Work area from entrance
  7  Entrance area
  8  Diagonal corridors from entrance area
Photo credit: Norman McGrath

**Schiller, DuCanto & Fleck Law Offices**
**Chicago, Illinois**
Environ, Inc., Architecture, Design & Planning
  9  Reception area featuring Italian marble
 10  Main conference room featuring
     oriental artwork
Photo credit: Anthony May Studio

9

10

1

2

3

**Alliance of American Insurers**
**Downers Grove, Illinois**
Environ, Inc., Architecture, Design & Planning
1   Reception area featuring Italian marble and
    cherry wood detailing
2   Comfortable and functional
    conference room
3   Internal office space
4   An efficient work environment
Photo credit: Anthony May Studio

4

1

2

**ICG Communications Corporate Campus
Englewood, Colorado**
Fentress Bradburn Architects
Design Architect: Steven Wood Architects

1 Custom-designed, period reproduction executive office
2 Private reception area, conference room for executive office
3 Full-service employee caféteria

4 Hall leading to executive wing featuring vintage photographs
5 Atrium for formal and casual gatherings
6 Custom-made furniture and coffered ceiling of executive conference room
7 Custom-made executive assistant desks
8 Service reliability center
9 Executive reception area with distinctive skylight for abundant daylighting

Photo credit: Nick Merrick

3

4

5

6

7

8

9

3

4

2

5

6

7

**One Union Street Seismic Retrofit**
**San Francisco, California**
Huntsman Architectural Group

Opposite:
New lobby with original wood columns
2    After renovation
Photo credit: Sharon Risendorph

**Gitlen Law Office**
**Santa Monica, California**
Kanner Architects

3    Detail of glass enveloped entry that rotates out from existing building façade
4    Street front façade of the adaptive reuse 1920's brick building
5    Detail of center stairway flanked by offices that offset from one another
6    Entry lobby and reception area
7    Upper level offices are set around atrium space punctured by a simple steel and wood stair
Photo credit: courtesy Kanner Architects

1

2

3

**Barney Skanska Construction
Company Offices
New York, New York**
Fox & Fowle Architects

1    Daylight pours into open office area due to
     translucent panels along exterior
2    Translucent, interduct telephone and data
     wiring arch from mill-finish aluminum cable
     trays to top of workstations, creating a
     practical design solution
3    President's office
Photo credit: David Joseph courtesy Fox & Fowle
Architects

**Muir, Cornelius, Moore
New York, New York**
Alfredo De Vido Architects

4    Reception
5    Conference room
Photo credit: Paul Warchol

**Epoch Films
Beverly Hills, California**
Kappe Studio

6    Interior street
Photo credit: courtesy Kappe Studio

**Harris Trust and Savings Bank
Chicago, Illinois**
Loebl Scholssman & Hackl

7    Reception area
Photo credit: Bruce VanInwegen

4

5

6

9

10

**Harris Trust and Savings Bank**
**Chicago, Illinois**
Loebl Scholssman & Hackl
Previous pages:
    Teaming areas
 9   Reception lobby
10  Teaming areas
11  Contoured corridor
12  Open spaces and workstations
13  Reception lobby
Photo credit: Bruce VanInwegen

11

12

13

**Gulf Canada Resources Limited**
**Denver, Colorado**
Fentress Bradburn Architects

Previous pages:
　　Reception area
2　Executive conference room
3　Custom-built stairway of steel, wood and
　　leather
4　Executive corridor featuring world's largest
　　collection of Winchester guns
Opposite:
　　Employee lounge
Photo credit: Nick Merrick

2

3

4

**Marmon Mok Corporate Office**
**San Antonio, Texas**
Marmon Mok

1   View toward project display gallery
2   View toward reception desk and
     elevator lobby
3   View toward reception desk and
     waiting area
Photo credit: Paul Bardagjy

**Adobe Systems Regional Headquarters**
**Quadrant Lake Union Center**
**Seattle, Washington**
NBBJ

4   Caféteria
5   Conference rooms/lounge spaces
6   Main entry/elevator lobby
Photo credit: Assassi Productions

**Lobby Renovation, 108 East 16th Street**
**New York, New York**
Alfredo De Vido Architects

7   Exterior
8   Interior view
Photo credit: courtesy Alfredo De Vido Architects

**Concert Commerce Park**
**Reston, Virginia**
RTKL Associates Inc.

9   View inside private, 'visually translucent'
     meeting rooms
10  View of open teaming area with
     visual privacy
Photo credit: Maxwell MacKenzie

4

5

6

7

8

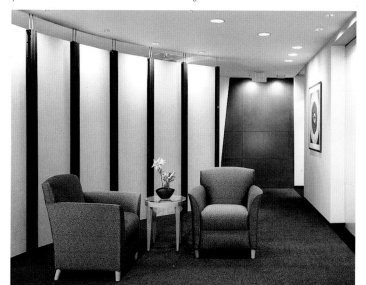

9

10

1

**First Place Tower**
**Tulsa, Oklahoma**
Loebl Schlossman & Hackl

1    Custom-designed elevator lobby
Photo credit: Hedrich-Blessing

**Millbrook Business Center**
**Lincolnshire/Buffalo Grove, Illinois**
Loebl Schlossman & Hackl

2    Second floor reception lobby
3    Grand stairway entry
Photo credit: Bruce VanInwegen

2

3

**State Street Lafayette Corporate Center**
**Boston, Massachusetts**
Sasaki Associates Inc.
1　View of servery
2　General open plan uses 85% indirect light
3　Reception suite offers clients a private
　　setting
4　Interior core incorporates break station
　　and color
Photo credit: Edward Jacoby

2

3

4

**State Street Lafayette Corporate Center**
**Boston, Massachusetts**
Sasaki Associates Inc.

5 Custom table and credenza are data smart
6 Corporate branding integrates
   into architecture
7 Dining and presentation room
8 Curved plexiglass panels are edge-lit
Opposite:
   Presentation room uses latest audio-visual
Photo credit: Edward Jacoby

5

6

7

8

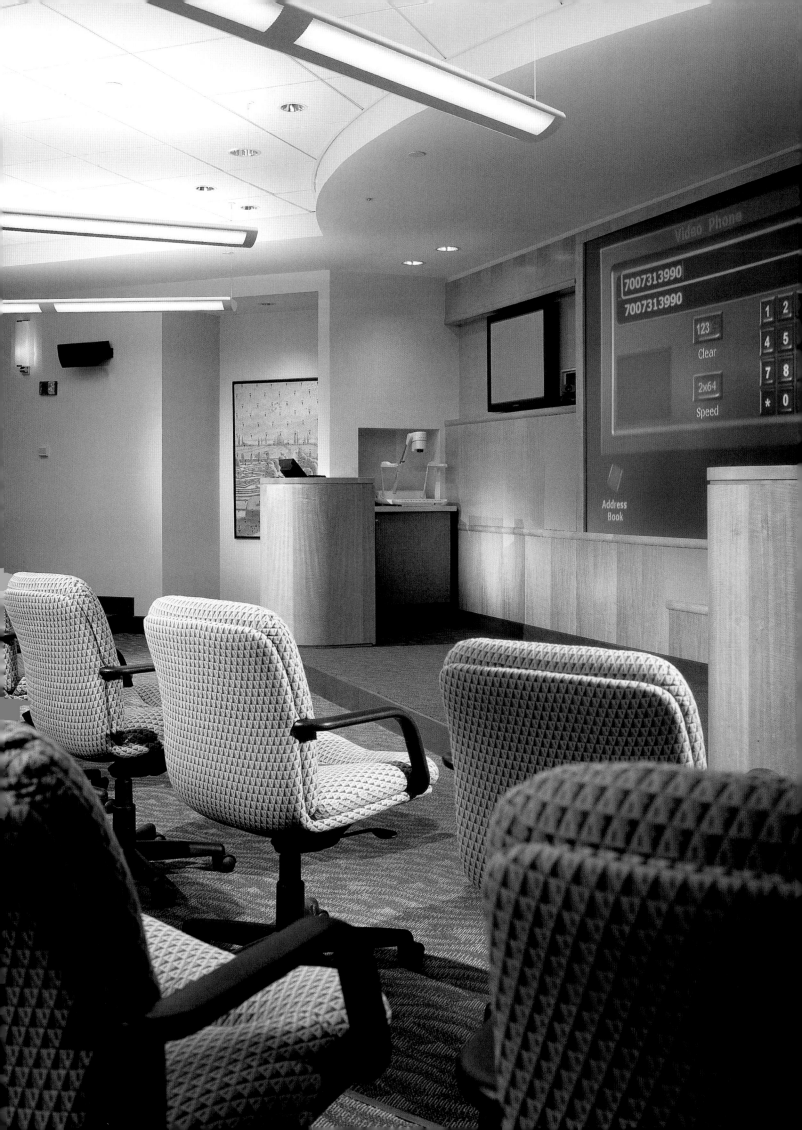

**Simpson Investment**
**Seattle, Washington**
NBBJ

1 Stairs leading to work area
2 Lunch/break area
3 Detail shot of staircase
4 Corridor in work area
Photo credit: Assassi Productions

**Raleigh - Durham Airport Authority**
**Raleigh, North Carolina**
Pearce Brinkley Cease + Lee Architects

5&6 View of entry canopy
7 View of entry
8 View of lobby looking north
9 View of lobby looking south
Photo credit: James West

1

2

3

4

5

6

7

8

9

10

11

12

**Raleigh - Durham Airport Authority**
**Raleigh, North Carolina**
Pearce Brinkley Cease + Lee Architects
Opposite:
    View of main stairs
10    View of lobby toward entry
Photo credit: James West

**1333 New Hampshire NW**
**Washington, DC**
RTKL Associates Inc.

11    Top-lit glass canopies express recessed
       elevator entrances
12    Vaulted panels and recesses break up
       expansive ceiling
Photo credit: Maxwell MacKenzie

**The Attik Corporate Office**
**San Francisco, California**
Rose Architecture

1   Interior view of conference room
2   View of workspace, lounge and conference room
3   View of workstation
4   View at conference room entry
5   View of lobby and reception area from entry
Photo credit: Richard Barnes

**William M. Mercer - WRG**
**Washington, DC**
RTKL Associates Inc.

6   View of suite entry and signage
7   View of reception desk framed by textured wall
Photo credit: Maxwell MacKenzie

1

2

3

4

5

6

7

1

2

3

4

**Teledesic**
**Bellevue, Washington**
NBBJ

1   Main waiting area
2   Open office area, main floor
3   Office corridor
4   Stairs to mezzanine
Photo credit: Steve Keating

**Suttle Mindlin Design Studio Space**
**St. Louis, Missouri**
SUTTLE MINDLIN

5   Design studio contributes to 'life in the city'
Photo credit: Alise O'Brien Architectural
Photography

**Edelman Public Relations**
**Washington, DC**
RTKL Associates Inc.

6   Sliding suite entry door at reception
7   Fabric panels with suspended glass logo at
    reception
8   Curvilinear bulkhead and freestanding
    counter in lunchroom
Photo credit: Maxwell MacKenzie

5

6

7

8

1

2

3

4

**Monitor Company**
**Cambridge, Massachusetts**
Sasaki Associates Inc.

1   View of work atrium
2   Client reception area
3   Client break-out area with boardroom
    in background
4   Corridor at service node in
    consultant neighborhood
5   Consultant mailboxes

Photo credit: Edward Jacoby

5

**7 Summits**
**Beverly Hills, California**
Steven Ehrlich Architects

1   Reception area, conference zone pivoting
    door open
2   Reception area, conference pivot doors open
3   Custom conference table
4   General work zone
5   Principal's office, sliding panel
Photo credit: Marvin Rand

**Southland Communities**
**Aliso Viejo, California**
Ted Wells Mark Noble, Inc

6   Steel walled conference room and custom
    plywood light fixture
7   Translucent fabric walls, plywood
    workstations, polished concrete floors
Photo credit: Glenn Cormier courtesy Ted Wells
Mark Noble, Inc.

**Virgin Atlantic Clubhouse**
**Dulles, Virginia**
RTKL Associates Inc.

1   View of main bar showing stairs
    to mezzanine
2   View of lounge showing curved accent walls
3   Terrace area with bar and stairs to
    mezzanine beyond
4   Floor-to-ceiling windows enhance view in
    main dining area
Photo credit: Maxwell MacKenzie

1

2                                                      3

**Monitor Clipper Partners**
**Cambridge, Massachusetts**
Sasaki Associates Inc.

1   View of kitchen overlooking atrium
2   Administrative stations outside private offices
3   View down office corridor to presentation room
Photo credit: Edward Jacoby

2

3

1         2         3

4         5         6

**Hines Offices**
**Santa Monica, California**
Steven Ehrlich Architects

1   Reception area, conference room to right
2   Conference room from reception area
3   Conference room with table
4   Corridor with metal 'blades' partitions
5   Typical metal 'blades' office interior
6   Metal 'blades' slicing across office
Photo credit: Jonathan Dewdney

**DMB&B Advertising Agency Interior**
**Renovation and Respositioning**
**St. Louis, Missouri**
SUTTLE MINDLIN

7&8   An enhanced sense of creativity for
staff interaction and client
presentations
Photo credit: Alise O'Brien Architectural
Photography

7

1

2

3

4

**DMB&B Advertising Agency Interior Renovation and Respositioning**
**St. Louis, Missouri**
**SUTTLE MINDLIN**

Opposite:
    'Urban loft' used as creative
    business strategy
Photo credit: Alise O'Brien Architectural
Photography

**California Teachers' Association (CTA) Headquarters**
**Burlingame, California**
**STUDIOS Architecture**

1    Central stair is focal point of building
2    State-of-the-art executive boardroom
3    View of central atrium
4    Reception area
Photo credit: Michael O'Callahan

**Calyx & Corolla Headquarters**
**San Francisco, California**
**STUDIOS Architecture**

Following pages:
    Lobby and reception area of mail-order
    flower company
Photo credit: Michael O'Callahan

1

2

3

4

**Calyx & Corolla Headquarters**
**San Francisco, California**
STUDIOS Architecture

1   Cutout allows conference room users
    a view of current product offerings
2   Conference room features witty details
3   Conference room is adjacent to
    demonstration area and call center
4   Staff dining area
5   20-foot long window floods call center with
    natural light

Photo credit: Michael O'Callahan

5

1

2

3

4

**Japan Foundation**
**Toronto, Canada**
Yabu Pushelberg

1  Reception area
2  Detail of transition area to foundation amenities
3  Open passageway from reception to lecture area
Photo credit: Robert Burley

**E*Trade Headquarters**
**Menlo Park, California**
STUDIOS Architecture

4  Break-out area and coffee bar
5  Lobby and reception area
6  Sloping and curving walls create dynamic workspace
Photo credit: Vittoria Visuals

5

6

**E*Trade Headquarters**
**Menlo Park, California**
STUDIOS Architecture
7   Vertical circulation adjacent to meeting areas
8   Network Control Center
Photo credit: Vittoria Visuals

1

2

3

4

**Centropolis Effects Interiors**
**Culver City, California**
Steven Ehrlich Architects

1   Reception area, stairway to mezzanine
2   Main street, principals' offices, stairway
     to mezzanine
3   Stair landing at mezzanine clerestory,
     custom light fixture
4   Main street, president's office,
     scheduling stations
Photo credit: Marvin Rand

**Marconi Communications**
**Valley Technology Center**
**San Jose, California**
STUDIOS Architecture

5   Break-out space on second floor
6   Cascading main stair features translucent
     plastic guardrail
Photo credit: Michael O'Callahan

5

6

7

**Marconi Communications
Valley Technology Center
San Jose, California**
STUDIOS Architecture

7   Industrial strip lighting marches along
    canted wall
8   Double height visitors' entry features
    industrial finishes
9   Wood panels add warmth to lobby area
Photo credit: Michael O'Callahan

**Sotheby's
New York, New York**
Swanke Hayden Connell Architects
Following pages:
    Board room
 Photo credit: Peter Aaron/Esto

8

9

**Sotheby's**
**New York, New York**
Swanke Hayden Connell Architects

1   Expert area
2   View of auction room from private viewing room
3   Cyber station
4   Waiting area/reception
Photo credit: Peter Aaron/Esto

**GFT Mode Canada**
**Toronto, Canada**
Yabu Pushelberg

5   Translucent enclosed offices
Photo credit: Robert Burley

3

5

4

1

2

3

4

**STUDIOS Architecture Renovation**
**San Francisco, California**
STUDIOS Architecture

1   Detail of wood and metal structure housing copy and storage area
2   Detail of glass and steel conference room door
3   Remnants of former paint warehouse remain untouched
4   Working garage door rises to create all-hands meeting area
5   View of conference room and custom wood detail
6   Reception area is juxtaposition of steel, wood, glass, plastic, aluminum, wire, and concrete

Photo credit: Michael O'Callahan

5

6

**GFT Mode Canada**
**Toronto, Canada**
Yabu Pushelberg
1   Reception area
2   General workstations
3   Interior of private offices
Photo credit: Robert Burley

**Charles Schwab**
**San Francisco, California**
STUDIOS Architecture
4   State-of-the-art video conference room
5   Typical conference room
6   Custom-designed glazed interior wall
Photo credit: Vittoria Visuals

1

2

3

4

5

7

8

9

10

11

12

13

15

16

**e-Citi**
**New York, New York**
Swanke Hayden Connell Architects

15    Lavatory
16    Informal conference area
17    Conference room
Photo credit: Peter Aaron/Esto

84

17

1

2

3

**3Com Corporate Briefing
& Training Center
Rolling Meadows, Illinois**
STUDIOS Architecture

1 Reception desk in main atrium
2 Reception desk and waiting area in
main atrium
3 View of briefing and training center
4 Reception desk and display wall in briefing
and training center
5 Detail of reception desk in briefing and
training center
6 Multipurpose room
Photo credit: Craig Dugan/Hedrich-Blessing

4

5

6

**CIBC/Wood Gundy Offices**
**Toronto, Ontario, Canada**
Kuwabara Payne McKenna Blumberg
1    Detail of glazed screen in reception area
2    Detail of east wall in President's office
Following pages:
     View of reception and waiting area, with artwork
     'The Jack Photographs' by John Massey 1992–95
Photo credit: Design Archive/Robert Burley

**CIBC/Wood Gundy Offices**
**Toronto, Ontario, Canada**
Kuwabara Payne McKenna Blumberg
Opposite:
 Meeting room with view of skyline looking north, with artwork 'Moraine' by Robert Fones, 1987
5  Detail of glazed wall along 'art spine'
Photo credit: Design Archive/Robert Burley

6

7

8

**CIBC/Wood Gundy Offices**
**Toronto, Ontario, Canada**
Kuwabara Payne McKenna Blumberg
6    View of President's private office with view of Lake Ontario
7    View along 'art spine' or central corridor
8    View of reception desk and foyer
Photo credit: Design Archive/Robert Burley

Commercial Space and Atria **95**

# Hospitality Space and Restaurants

**Monsoon Restaurant**
**Toronto, Canada**
Yabu Pushelberg

1    Bar length with lounge area to side
2    View looking into main dining areas
Photo credit: Evan Dion

1

2

3

4

5

6

7

8

9

10

**Westin Grand Hotel**
**Washington, DC**
NBBJ

3    Restaurant
4    Main lobby/reception area
5    Guest room with storage and wardrobe unit
6    Elevator lobby
7    Guest room
8    Restaurant
Photo credit: Assassi Productions

**Star Bar**
**Chicago Illinois**
Environ, Inc. Architecture, Design & Planning

9    An elegant atmosphere greets patrons
10   Lounge provides warm, comfortable
      setting
Photo credit: Anthony May Studio

**Lofts**
**Columbus, Ohio**
NBBJ

1   Guest room with steel and wood detailing
2   Executive suite features custom designed furnishings
3   Interiors feature custom designed furnishings
4   Lobby, main entrance
5   Custom designed steel and wood reception desk
Photo credit: Kirk Fisher - Imagemakers Photographic

**Club Hotel by Doubletree, Boston Bayside**
**Boston Massachusetts**
Arrowstreet Inc.

6   Club room is a gracious combination of luxury and efficiency
7   Custom artwork (by Joe Zena) invests club room with personality
8   Colors and textures in lobby echo hotel's seaside location
Photo credit: Robert E. Mikrut

1

2

3

4

5

6

7

8

1

2

3

4

5

**Edmond Meany Hotel**
**Seattle, Washington**
NBBJ
1   Main lobby entrance and seating area
2   Main lobby/waiting reception area
3   Coffee bar
4&5 Guest room
6   News café, cigar case
7   Main lobby/ballroom seating area
Photo credit: Assassi Production

6

7

Leisure and Art Centers

**Atlantis Alliance-The Beach**
**Toronto, Canada**
Yabu Pushelberg
1   Lobby/concession
2   Café reading bar
Photo credit: Evan Dion

**Omaha Civic Auditorium Renovation**
**Omaha, Nabraska**
Leo A Daly
3   Music Hall
Photo credit: Paul Brokering

**Green Door Spa**
**St. Louis, Missouri**
SUTTLE MINDLIN
Opposite:
    Hospitality and 'sanctuary' for luxury spa
Photo credit: Alise O'Brien Architectural Photography

1

2

3

**Green Door Spa**
**St. Louis, Missouri**
SUTTLE MINDLIN

4&5    A focused expression of this customer's llifestyle
Photo credit: Alise O'Brien Architectural Photography

**University of Maryland Campus Recreation Center**
**College Park, Maryland**
Sasaki Architecture Inc.

Following pages:
    View of information desk at main entrance
Photo credit: Christopher Barnes

Conference Room · Racquetball/Squash · West Gym

**University of Maryland Campus Recreation Center**
**College Park, Maryland**
Sasaki Architecture Inc.
Opposite:
    View of primary circulation spine
1   View of gymnasium with suspended jogging track
2   Cardiovascular work-out area
3   Details of facility's pool
4   View of facility's juice bar
Photo credit: Christopher Barnes

1

2

3

4

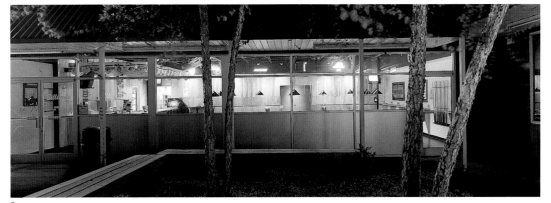

**University of Maryland Campus Recreation Center**
**College Park, Maryland**
Sasaki Architecture Inc.

5   View of main circulation spine
Photo credit: Christopher Barnes

**Sunset Hills Billiards Hall**
**Raleigh, North Carolina**
Pearce Brinkley Cease + Lee Architects

6   View of exterior
7   View from billiards hall toward bar
8   View of architect designed cue rack
9   View from bar into billiards hall
Photo credit: James West

6

7

8

9

**J. J. Lally Chinese Art**
**New York, New York**
Alfredo De Vido Architects

1   Entry
2   Display cabinet
3   Interior view
4   Display cabinet
Photo credit: Norman McGrath

**Hoyts Cine 12 at Brass Mill Center**
**Waterbury, Connecticut**
Arrowstreet Inc.

5   Generating excitement through all
    three levels
6   Quickava/ticket point
7   Cinema as mall's third floor anchor
Photo credit: Robert E. Mikrut

**Muvico Theater**
**Davie, Florida**
Development Design Group

8   Concession/guest hall
Photo credit: Muvico Theaters

1

2

3

4

5

6

7

8

1

**Private Corporate Fitness Center**
**San Francisco, California**
Hendler Design
1   Snack bar
2   Private office with tufted wall
Following pages:
    Reception
Photo credit: David Wakely Photography

3

**Private Corporate Fitness Center**
**San Francisco, California**
Hendler Design

3    Shower room
4    Weight room
Photo credit: David Wakely Photography

4

5

**Private Corporate Fitness Center**
**San Francisco, California**
Hendler Design
5    Machines and administrative offices overlooking Jackson Square
6    Aerobics room
Photo credit: David Wakely Photography

6

1

**The Strategic Air Command Museum**
**Ashland, Nabraska**
Leo A Daly
1&2    Main entry atrium
Photo credit: Paul Brokering

2

**Westwood Country Club Dining
Facilities Renovation
St. Louis, Missouri**
Suttle Mindlin

1–4　Traditional setting for contemporary
　　　and gracious lifestyle
Photo credit: Alise O'Brien Architectural Photography,
David Dale Suttle for HOK

1

2

3

**Rainbow Babies Children's Hospital**
**Cleveland, Ohio**
NBBJ

1    Two-story public area
2    Main reception area
3    Patient room
4    Nursing area desk
5    Hospital corridor
Photo credit: Tim Hursley

**Crossroads Atrium**
**City of Industry, California**
WET Design

6–8    Laminar stream water sculpture
Photo credit: Mark Fuller

**Loyola University Medical Center**
**Stritch School of Medicine**
**Maywood, Illinois**
Ellenzweig Associates, Inc.

9    Main entrance lobby
Photo credit: George Lambros

1

2

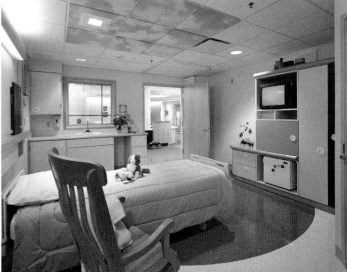

3

4

5

6

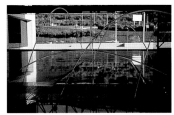

7

8

9

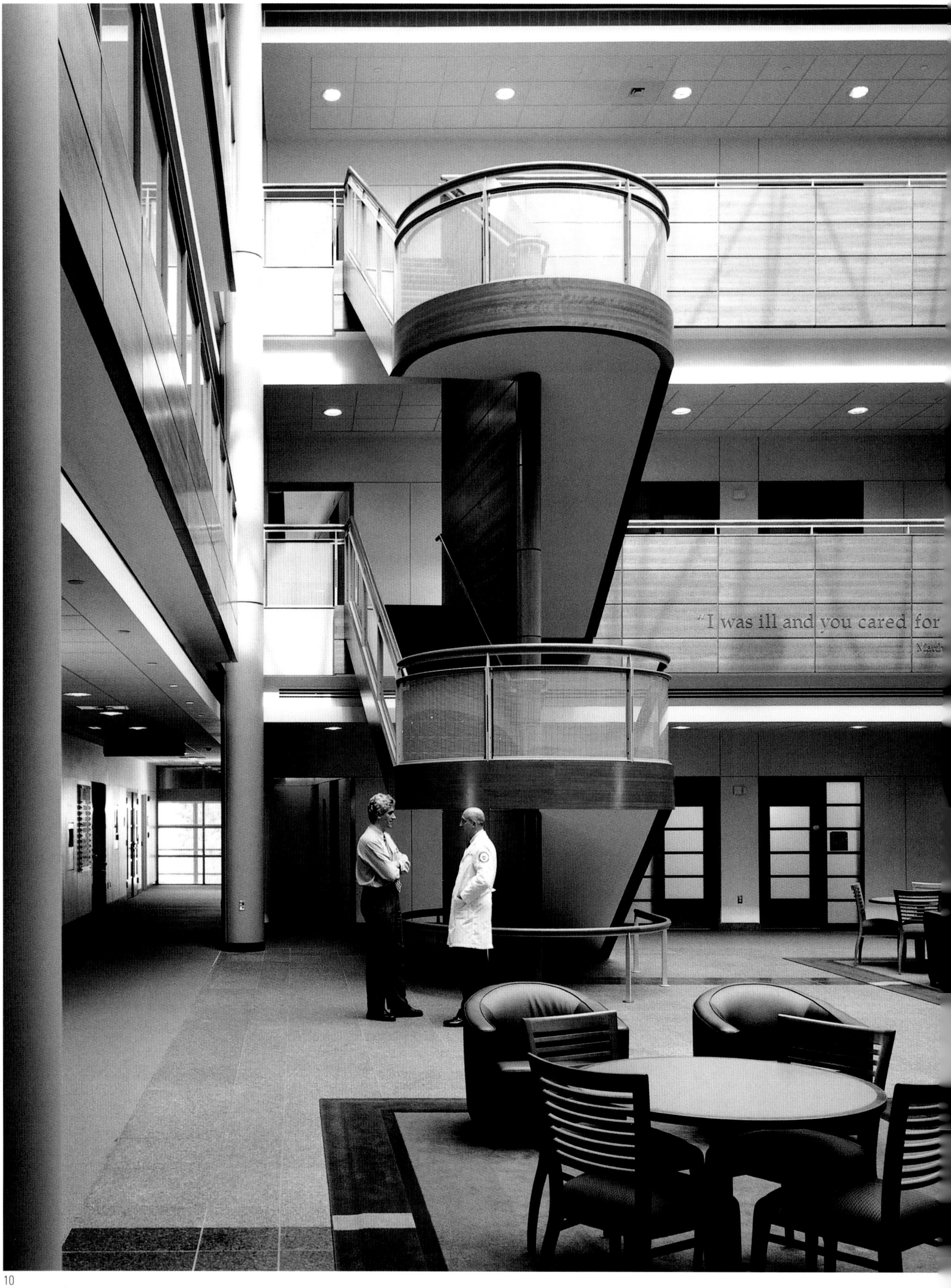
"I was ill and you cared for

**Loyola University Medical Center**
**Stritch School of Medicine**
**Maywood, Illinois**
Ellenzweig Associates, Inc.

10   Three-story sky-lit central commons atrium
11   Flexible learning cluster area
12   Tiered case-method classroom
13   Flat-floor classroom
Photo credit: George Lambros (10, 11, 13); Hedrich-Blessing (12)

11

12

13

**Schaumburg Township District Library**
**Schaumburg, Illinois**
Phillips Swager Associates
Opposite:
    Children's area
1   Library café
2   Reading area
Photo credit: Paul Schlismann Photography (1);
Scott McDonald/Hedrich Blessing

1

2

3

4

5

**Schaumburg Township District Library**
**Schaumburg, Illinois**
Phillips Swager Associates

3   Second floor reference area
4   Lobby
5   Second floor elevator area

Photo credit: Paul Schlismann Photography (1); Scott McDonald/Hedrich Blessing

1

2

3

4

**McCormick Convention Center
Expansion Water Feature
Chicago, Illinois**
WET Design

1–4    Interior atrium with kinetic water feature
Photo credit: Ira Kahn

**Swedish Medical Center
Seattle, Washington**
NBBJ

5    Ambulatory care playroom
6    Surgery recovery room with lighting
      levels creating calm atmosphere
7    Women and infant's LDRP room
8    Main lobby to13-block campus,
      intersection of major
      circulation corridors
9    Separaton between main lobby and
      ambulatory care waiting area
Photo credit: Assassi Productions and Steve Keating

**Exchange Conference Center
Boston, Massachusetts**
Arrowstreet Inc.

10    Upper level meeting space
11    Detail of 'porthole' ocular window
12    Grand hall presentation room
Photo credit: Robert E. Mikrut

5

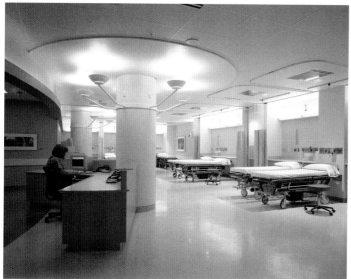

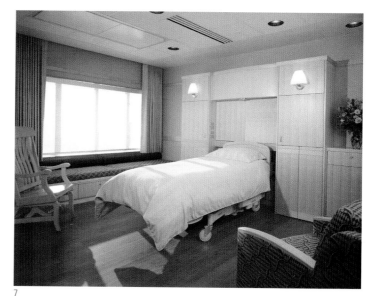

6

7

9

8

10

11

12

1

2

3

4

**Massachusetts Institute of Technology
Dorrance and Whitaker Buildings
Cambridge, Massachusetts**
Ellenzweig Associates, Inc.

1 Classroom entryway
2 Graphic display niche
3 Main lobby with terrazzo floor looking west
4 Flat-level classroom
5 Main lobby with fiber-optic edge-lit art glass
6 Main lobby with terrazzo floor looking east
Photo credit: Steve Rosenthal

5

6

7

**Massachusetts Institute of Technology**
**Dorrance and Whitaker Buildings**
**Cambridge, Massachusetts**
Ellenzweig Associates, Inc.

7    State-of-the-art athena computer cluster
Opposite:
     Fourth floor lobby
Photo credit: Steve Rosenthal

**Science Laboratory Buildling, Illinois State University**
**Normal, Illinois**
Loebl Schlossman & Hackl
Opposite:
　　　Four-story atrium entry
Photo credit: Scott McDonald, Hedrich-Blessing

**Chapel of Mt St Dominic**
**Caldwell, New Jersey**
Alfredo De Vido Architects
1&2　　Renovated chapel interior
Photo credit: Paul Warchol

**Gas Company Tower Water Feature**
**Los Angeles, California**
WET Design
3–5　　WaterUnderGlass ™ interior extends to outside plaza
Photo credit: Ira Kahn

**Ursinus College Science Facility**
**Collegeville, Pennsylvania**
Ellenzweig Associates, Inc.
Following pages:
　　　Lecture hall
Photo credit: Anton Grassl

1

**Ursinus College Science Facility**
**Collegeville, Pennsylvania**
Ellenzweig Associates, Inc
1   North atrium looking west
2   Chemistry teaching laboratory
3   Detail of communicating stair
Photo credit: Anton Grassl

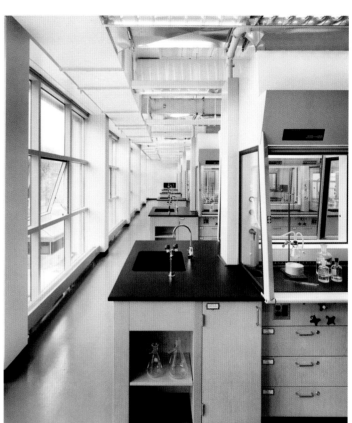

2

3

**Ursinus College Science Facility**
**Collegeville, Pennsylvania**
Ellenzweig Associates, Inc
4    North atrium looking east
Opposite:
    South atrium
Photo credit: Anton Grassl

**Easton Town Center**
**Columbus, Ohio**
Development Design Group

1    Entertainment zone
Photo credit: Walter Larrimore Photography

**Bowdoin College**
**Stanley F. Druckenmiller Hall**
**Brunswick, Maine**
Ellenzweig Associates, Inc.

2    Atrium staircase
3    Lobby with exhibit space
4    Sky-lit atrium
Photo credit: Steve Rosenthal

2

3

4

5

**Bowdoin College**
**Stanley F. Druckenmiller Hall**
**Brunswick, Maine**
Ellenzweig Associates, Inc.

5    Tiered classroom
6    Flexible teaching laboratory
Photo credit: Steve Rosenthal

6

Bowdoin College
Stanley F. Druckenmiller Hall
Brunswick, Maine
Ellenzweig Associates, Inc.
7   Two-story lobby
Opposite:
     Greenhouse
Photo credit: Steve Rosenthal

**Augustana College**
**Science Facility**
**Rock Island, Illinois**
Ellenzweig Associates, Inc
Opposite:
    Atrium detail
1   Three-story sky-lit atrium
Photo credit: Anton Grassl

1

2

**Augustana College**
**Science Facility**
**Rock Island, Illinois**
Ellenzweig Associates, Inc

2    Teaching laboratory
3    Hall and classroom entryway
Photo credit: Anton Grassl

**Chinese Cultural Center and Public Library**
**Scarborough, Ontario, Canada**
Kuwabara Payne McKenna Blumberg
in joint venture with Patrick T.Y., Chan,
Architects
Following pages:
    Detail of entrance to Festival Court
Photo credit: Kerun Ip, courtesy KPMB

3

1

2

**Chinese Cultural Center and Public Library**
**Scarborough, Ontario, Canada**
Kuwabara Payne McKenna Blumberg
in joint venture with Patrick T.Y., Chan,
Architects

1   Glass covered canopy outside main entry
2   Detail of ceiling in Festival Hall
Photo credit: Kerun Ip, courtesy KPMB

# Retail Space and Showrooms

1

2

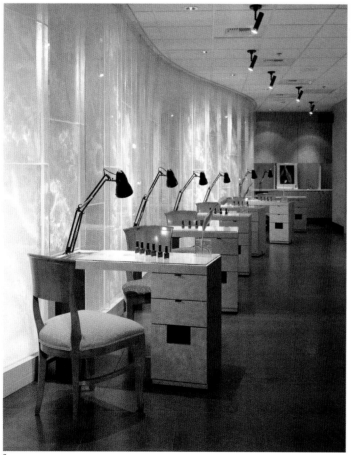

3

4

**Gene Juarez Salon & Spa**
**Seattle, Washington**
NBBJ

1&2  Upper level entrance gallery with cast glass wall
  3  Manicure area with cast glass wall
  4  Retail area with plaster wall display
  5  Hair salon stations with fabric wrapped light fixtures
Photo credit: Assassi Productions

**Gene Juarez Salon & Spa**
**Seattle, Washington**
NBBJ

  6  Upper level waiting area
  7  Day spa entrance with water feature
  8  Seating niche at entrance gallery
  9  Day spa corridor
Photo credit: Assassi Productions

5

6

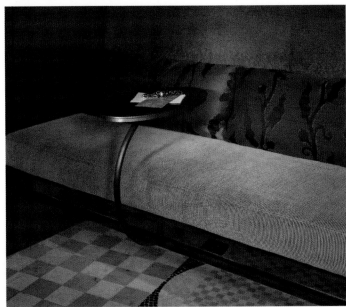

8

7

9

10

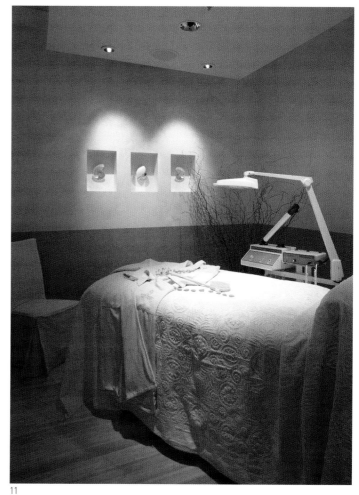

11

12

13

**Gene Juarez Salon & Spa**
**Seattle, Washington**
NBBJ

10   Spa waiting area with water feature
11   Spa treatment room
12   Vichy shower at day spa
13   Retail area
14   Retail with high bronze wall and
      transaction desk
15   Street level retail space with transparent
      image panels
16   Detail of day spa entrance
Photo credit: Assassi Productions

**Duty Free Shoppers, Los Angeles**
**International Airport**
**Los Angeles, California**
Leo A Daly
Following pages:
      Duty Free Shoppers
Photo credit: Eric Poppleton

14

15

16

**Holt Renfrew and Co. Ltd.:**
**Anne Klein Boutique**
**Toronto, Canada**
Yabu Pushelberg
1    Illuminated back-lit fibreglass wall
2    Custom alabaster chandelier
4    Anne Klein room wooden screen
Photo credit: Robert Burley

1

2

3

4

5

**A New Leaf Studio & Garden**
**Chicago, Illinois**
**Weese Langley Weese Architects**
3   Store creates a transition from street to garden
5   New glass block floor in garden illuminates basement
6   Stairs have tensioned steel cable railings and steel grate treads
7   New openings were created to basement space
Photo credit: © Karant + Associates

6

7

8

9

**A New Leaf Studio & Garden**
**Chicago, Illinois**
Weese Langley Weese Architects
8    Palette of industrial materials developed includes new steel stairs
9    New steel casement doors open to garden
Opposite:
     Spaces were gutted exposing original masonry openings
Photo credit: © Karant + Associates

**Guess! Rodeo**
**Beverly Hills, California**
Kanner Architects
Following pages:
     Detail of brushed stainless steel railing around self-supporting stairway
     finished in cherry wood
Photo credit: courtesy Kanner Architects

**Guess! Rodeo**
**Beverly Hills, California**
Kanner Architects

2   Clean, retro-modernist fixtures greet customers at stainless steel and glass storefront entry
3   Minimalist fixtures composed of stainless steel, glass, and cherry act to showcase and not overpower the merchandise
4   Striking interior design focuses attention on featured merchandise and trademark advertising graphics of Guess?

Photo credit: courtesy Kanner Architects

2

3

4

**Crestwood Mall Renovation**
**St. Louis, Missouri**
SUTTLE MINDLIN
1&Opposite:
    How to be effective...on a budget
Photo credit: Alise O'Brien Architectural
Photography

**Café Nishiki**
**Los Angeles, California**
Steven Ehrlich Architects

1   Main dining space
2   Entry sequence
3   Tower, booth below, private dining above
4   New sushi counter with canopy above
5   Udon counter, sushi bar and tower beyond
6   Main dining area
Photo credit: Jonathan Dewdney

**Hong Kong Economics & Trade Office**
**Washington, DC**
Leo A Daly

7   Reception area
8   Stairwell
Photo credit: Maxwell MacKenzie

1

2

3

4

5

6

7

**Roadrunner Casino**
**Henderson, Nevada**
NBBJ

1 Mini-casino, bar/lounge, restaurant/dining room, pool hall area
2 Bar/lounge, restaurant area, and dance floor spaces
3 Restaurant and dining room area
4 Mini-casino
5 Bar/lounge
Photo credit: Michael Shopenn

**Art of the Past**
**New York, New York**
Alfredo De Vido Architects

6 Cabinetry and lighting designed by the architect
7 200-square-foot shop selling Indian art
Photo credit: Norman McGrath

**Mikimoto, The Venetian Hotel & Casino**
**Las Vegas, Nevada**
AM Partners, Inc.

8 Invokes the feeling of looking up to surface of sea
Photo credit: Jud Haggard

1

2

3

4

5

6

7

8

**Holt Renfrew and Co. Ltd.: Left Bank**
**Toronto, Canada**
Yabu Pushelberg
- 9   Dividing screen and display wall
- 10   Ceiling panel and downlighting

Photo credit: Robert Burley

**Mikimoto, The Venetian Hotel & Casino**
**Las Vegas, Nevada**
AM Partners, Inc.
- 11   Design intent was to create upmarket, museum-like environment
- 12   Teardrop lights and mirrors evoke clarity of the ocean
- 13   Gently curved forms interact to achieve natural fluid setting
- 14   Pearwood and frosted glass create feeling of richness

Photo credit: Jud Haggard

9           10

12

13

14

**Kate's Paperie**
**New York, New York**
Alfredo De Vido Architects

1 Front of store features 'paper glass' front which is backlit with fibre optics
2&3 6,000 square-foot shop specializing in the sale of fine paper
4&5 Architect designed fixtures, lighting and paper ceiling

Photo credit: Norman McGrath

1

2

3

4

5

6

**Foodland Supermarket**
**Ewa Beach, Hawaii**
AM Partners, Inc.

6    Each department consists of customized
     signage and custom displays
7    Skylights provide natural lighting for
     energy efficiency
8    Design concept was 'Fun-Filled Family
     Marketplace'
Photo credit: Augie Salbosa

7

8

9

10

11

12

13

14

15

16

17

1

2

3

4

5

**Gene Juarez Salon & Spa**
**Redmond, Washington**
NBBJ

1 Spa waiting area with water feature
2 Day spa corridor with water feature
3 Hair salon cutting stations
4 Retail area and transaction desk
5 Waiting area
Photo credit: Assassi Productions

**Warehouse Row**
**Chattanooga, Tennessee**
Development Design Group

6 Main retail gallery
Photo credit: Steve Hogben Architectural
Photographics

6

1

2

3

4

5

6

7

8

9

1

2

3

4

5

6

7

8

9

**ULTA Cosmetics Fragrance Salon**
**Las Colinas, Irving, Texas**
Fitzpatrick Design Group, Inc.

1 'Boulevard' at store entrance features the color library
2 Major service center is centered in the space
3 Perimeter merchandise is organized by bold horizontal bands
4 Café invites customers to linger and relax
Photo credit: Whitney Cox Photographer 1999

**La Pelle**
**Honolulu, Hawaii**
AM Partners, Inc.

5 Design complements high quality merchandise
Photo credit: Augie Salbosa

**Word of Mouth/Café Word of Mouth**
**New York, New York**
Alfredo De Vido Architects

6 Entrance
7 Architect designed furniture
8&9 Street view
Photo credit: courtesy Alfredo De Vido Architects

**Lebanon Co-op Food Store**
**Lebanon, New Hampshire**
Arrowstreet Inc.

10 Recycled and reusable materials in earth-friendly store
11 Emphasis on natural light and traditional building techniques
12 Spectacular octagonal cupola
Photo credit: Robert E. Mikrut

10

11

12

**Maplewood Mall**
**Maplewood, Minnesota**
Development Design Group
1   Central court
Photo credit: courtesy Development Design Group

**Bon Marche BONsport Activewear Shop**
**Seattle, Washington**
Fitzpatrick Design Group, Inc.
2   Flexible fixturing allows strong vendor presentation
3   Photomurals on perimeter reflect store location
4   L.E.D. and graphic floor patterns draw customer attention
5   Heroically scaled photomural arches overhead
Photo credit: Robert Pisano Photography 1999

1

2

3

4

5

6

7

**La Chausseria**
**Manhattan, New York**
Alfredo De Vido Architects

6   Interior view
7   Exterior view
Photo credit: Fred Charles

**Collins & Aikman Showroom**
**New York, New York**
Fox & Fowle Architects, P.C.

8   Space begins with dramatic interior
    reception area that leads to large,
    light-filled showroom and
    conference space
Following pages:
    Showroom includes mobile display
    cabinets designed to house product
    portfolios on one side and flat art work
    on other side
Photo credit: David Sundberg/Esto

8

**Collins & Aikman Showroom**
**New York, New York**
Fox & Fowle Architects, P.C.
    Conference room is visually and physically
    connected to showroom
Photo credit: David Sundberg/Esto

**Marketplace at Oviedo Crossing**
**Oviedo, Florida**
ELS Elbasani & Logan Architects
Following pages:
    Exterior at night
Photo credit: Timothy Hursley

**Marketplace at Oviedo Crossing**
**Oviedo, Florida**
ELS Elbasani & Logan Architects
1   Food court overlooking garden
2   Food court
Opposite:
     Interior street
Photo credit: Timothy Hursley

1

2

**Marketplace at Oviedo Crossing**
**Oviedo, Florida**
ELS Elbasani & Logan Architects
3   Food court
4   Entry near cinemas
Photo credit: Timothy Hursley

# Biographies

### Abo•Copeland Architecture, Inc.
### Denver, Colorado

Abo•Copeland Architecture, Inc., Denver, Colorado, is a medium-sized firm specializing in laboratory, office, education, and residential design. Founded in 1994, the firm is dedicated to bringing excellence in both service and design to the Rocky Mountain region.

Each of the partners is recognized for particular expertise developed over a 30-year span in the profession. Ronald K. Abo is an expert in historic preservation and holds numerous awards for his architecture. John W. Priebe is a specialist in laboratory design. Stephen K. Loos has won awards for his designs of both large and small projects. Daniel Cervantes' talents lie in quality production and project management.

Current projects include national and international pharmaceutical 'clean' laboratories, renewable energy laboratories for the development of photovoltaic and wind energy usage, office buildings, public and private schools along the Front Range, higher education facilities for high-technology research and development, and large-scale urban housing redevelopment in Denver.

### Blauel Architects
### London, United Kingdom

Formed in 1986, Blauel Architects has achieved a reputation for innovative designs for offices, private and public housing, cafés, banks and shops, showing an ability to carry out work in different national contexts. The work demonstrates imaginative use of space and a concern for the most economical application of suitable materials combined with the application of modern building techniques.

Commissions recently completed include a working environment for an internet access provider in California, various contracts for the German Foreign Office, headquarters for two European banks and a corporate fit-out in the IFC-Tower 42 in the City of London, fashion shops and offices in the West End of London, a contemporary gallery in Birmingham funded by the Arts Council and work for private clients in the UK, Germany, Italy and Switzerland.

### Development Design Group, Inc.
### Baltimore, Maryland

Design Group is a leading international architecture, planning and design firm with a history of creating high profile, high quality environments around the world.

Design Group's vast portfolio includes exciting new retail and entertainment concepts, first-class hotel, leisure, and resort facilities, unique office and residential designs, and large mixed-use destinations offering a range of elements and activities. A host of prestigious international clients seeks Design Group's multi-disciplinary professional services for themed environments, entertainment/retail, regional planning, waterfront development, urban and suburban revitalization, specialty center development, and creative concept generation for land use and project feasibility on every imaginable scale and scope—and in every corner of the globe.

Design Group's multilingual teams create internationally successful projects from the firm's Baltimore, Maryland (USA) headquarters, and from offices in Asia, Africa, Europe and the Middle East. Design Group's team of professionals have extensive experience in virtually every aspect of development. With extensive experience in retail, entertainment, graphics, planning, town centers, hospitality and mixed-use projects, Design Group commands diverse resources to create places that are harmoniously integrated with their surroundings and culturally attuned to the lifestyles of clients and their customers.

## Ellenzweig Associates, Inc.
## Cambridge, Massachusetts

Ellenzweig Associates specializes in complex, technically challenging projects—teaching laboratories, research laboratories and classroom spaces for higher education; research facilities for biomedical and biotechnology clients; and infrastructure facilities and parking structures for various clients. Initial and continuing laboratory commissions at Harvard University and MIT launched the firm's longstanding focus on projects for higher education and research institutions. The firm was established 35 years ago, is located in Cambridge, Massachusetts, and has a total staff of over 60.

The firm's commitment to design excellence and client satisfaction is reflected in commissions at many distinguished institutions. Recent or current clients include Harvard University, Massachusetts Institute of Technology, University of Chicago, Stanford University, University of Virginia, Johns Hopkins University, University of Pennsylvania, Loyola University Medical Center, Dartmouth College, Bryn Mawr College, Bowdoin College, Children's Hospital of Philadelphia, and Children's Hospital of Boston.

Ellenzweig Associates has won over 70 design awards, including a 1999 Special Citation from the Boston Society of Architects (BSA) for Loyola University Stritch School of Medicine; two AIA New England 1996 Honor Awards for Design Excellence for MIT Sloan School's Tang Center for Management Education and MIT's Cogeneration Plant; a 1996 Honor Award for Architecture from the American Institute of Architects (AIA) for the Joslin Diabetes Center; a 1995 *R&D Magazine* Lab of the Year Special Mention (also for Joslin); and a 1994 AIA Honor Award for Urban Design for Post Office Square. For Post Office Square, the firm was also honored with the BSA's 1992 Harleston Parker Medal for the most beautiful architecture in Boston.

Our science and laboratory projects are recognized for their technical know-how, design excellence, successful engineering coordination, economy, efficiency, and perhaps most of all, for their humanity. We understand that students, faculty, and researchers spend long hours in their laboratory workspaces, and we pay a great deal of attention to making these laboratories safe, well-lit, well-organized, and delightful spaces in which to teach and work. We understand also that laboratory activities are aided by interaction and cross-fertilization among individuals, and we look for opportunities in building layouts to provide convenient yet economical spaces for this activity. We recognize that science buildings must function well on a variety of levels, including technical, aesthetic, operational, and environmental; first of all, however, they must be wonderful places for the people who spend so much of their time there.

## Fentress Bradburn Architects
## Denver, Colorado

Since 1980, Fentress Bradburn Architects has practiced innovative, client-driven, technologically advanced architecture and interiors in locations throughout the world.

Fentress Bradburn's design work is noted as much for its aesthetics as for its pragmatic method of fulfilling program. The firm's design philosophy focuses on tying a building to its region as well as to its context, always striving foremost to meet the needs of the end user and to create harmony between the exterior and interior of a building.

From its initial high-rise office projects begun in 1980 to Fentress Bradburn's current design role as associate architect with HNTB Sports in creating the new Denver Broncos NFL football stadium, diversity has been a hallmark of the firm's work. Projects have ranged from airports and office buildings to convention centers, museums and government facilities, not only throughout the United States but also in Asia, the Middle East and Latin America.

Fentress Bradburn has won over 140 design awards and citations, including three national awards from the American Institute of Architects, the Architecture and Energy Award for the General Services Administration's Natural Resources Building in Olympia, Washington, and the United States Department of Transportation's Design Honor Award for Denver International Airport. The firm has also won 13 national and international design competitions, including airports in Seoul, Korea, and Doha, Qatar, and public facilities in Oakland, California, and Las Vegas, Nevada.

With more than 10 million square feet of interior space completed, Fentress Bradburn is currently ranked among the top 150 firms in the *Interior Design Giants List*. Clients include Lucent Technologies, ICG Communications, J.D. Edwards & Co., Citicorp/Diners Club, IBM, Apple Computer, Gulf Canada Resources, the Denver Art Museum, the General Services Administration and American Television & Communications.

## Marmon Mok
## San Antonio, Texas

Marmon Mok was established in 1953 in San Antonio, Texas and has grown to become one of the state's largest architectural and engineering firms with a staff of over 60.

The firm is directed by six partners that oversee six studios. These studios include: corporate/financial, healthcare/research, education/civic, government/industrial, engineering and interiors.

Marmon Mok's work ranges from a 4,400 square-foot branch bank facility to a 600,000 square-foot corporate headquarters. The firm's most significant projects include: San Antonio International Airport Terminal 1, the 65,000 seat AlamoDome, Grossman Cancer Center and Security Service Federal Credit Union corporate headquarters.

Marmon Mok's design approach considers the design process to be a rigorous search for an appropriate architectural solution that is based on the explorations of users' expressed aspirations and needs. As a highly participatory process , Marmon Mok regards the creation of architecture as an intensive and ongoing collaboration of clients, architects, engineers, and contractors.

### NBBJ
### Seattle, Washington

In 1943, four Seattle architects—Naramore, Bain, Brady and Johanson— joined forces to design a total support community for one of the nation's major shipyards. By pooling their talents and resources, they created the consummate architectural practice: a multi-specialty firm dedicated to providing quality design and superior service to its clients. The vision and values of these founding partners continue to guide NBBJ.

NBBJ believes that exceptional design adds value by faithfully reflecting an organization's identity. It emerges from and is created for the people, culture and spirit unique to each client's business. In this view, projects embody a distinct blend of diverse elements, balancing economic benefits, environmental assets and enduring architecture.

During the past 57 years, NBBJ has grown to become a global design practice committed to design excellence. Today it is the world's third largest architectural firm and the recipient of more than 300 national and international design awards. NBBJ has established strong specialty practices in design and consulting for: corporate, healthcare, sports and entertainment, airports, commercial, graphic design, higher education, justice, research and advanced technology, retail, senior living, and urban planning.

### Pearce Brinkely Cease + Lee, PA
### Raleigh, North Carolina

Pearce Brinkley Cease + Lee has the energy and optimism of a young firm supported by the experience and reputation of an established practice. Founded in 1945, the firm has built connections to the regional business community, government, and building trades which have helped them obtain a wide range of public and private sector projects. Their principals have matured with the firm, yet a majority of their design staff has joined the firm since 1993. This balance of experience and youth, pragmatism and idealism, shapes the firm's approach to every project.

As a firm, they are as equally diverse as their list of clients. With wide-ranging professional interests, talents and expertise, they can offer an array of complementary services: strategic planning, space planning, and programming; urban, architectural, and interior design; project management, and construction administration. Though large enough to provide the necessary scope of architectural services for a broad range of clients and building types, they stay small enough for their principals to be fully involved in every phase of a project.

Since the work the firm pursues varies dramatically in terms of building type and scale, they continue to expand both the breadth and depth of their experience. Their approach focuses on the uniqueness of each project rather than the development of a signature style for the firm. Recent projects include the RDU Center at Raleigh-Durham International Airport; renovations to the School of Journalism and Mass Communication at the University of North Carolina at Chapel Hill; renovations to both the East Campus Library and Divinity School Library at Duke University; an addition to the student center at Meredith College; and the addition of a new concert hall and theater to Memorial Auditorium, Raleigh's main performing arts center.

### STUDIOS Architecture
### San Francisco, California

STUDIOS Architecture is an international architecture, interiors, master planning and urban design firm founded in 1985. Their work is driven by ideas and stands out for its ability to transform corporate and civic values into a powerful physical experience. STUDIOS has offices in San Francisco, Los Angeles, Washington DC, New York, London, and Paris. The firm has been honored with more than 70 design awards and has been featured in more than 100 publications for its work around the world.

Current projects include the Milpitas City Hall in Silicon Valley, Wilson Cornerstone's 1 million square foot office campus development in downtown San Francisco, interiors for the Shanghai Grand Theatre, and projects worldwide for 3Com Corporation and SGI (formerly known as Silicon Graphics Computer Systems). Other clients include American Express, Nike, Excite@Home Inc., Andersen Consulting, AirTouch Communications, Charles Schwab, Tishman Speyer Properties, Cartoon Network, the Discovery Channel, Warner Bros., Sun Microsystems, E*Trade and Young and Rubicam.

## SUTTLE MINDLIN
### St. Louis, Missouri

SUTTLE MINDLIN is an international design studio headed by David Dale Suttle and Michael Mindlin, AIA. Through the firm's strategic approach to design and a recognized understanding of the marketplace, they work with their clients to promote their most enduring values. It is the search for a strategic beginning that has always been their best guarantee of success...a recognized process that has led the firm to decades of significant projects of acknowledged design excellence.

The practice is unique in its ability to help its client communicate to customers, employees, the marketplace, or the stock market. The firm is best known for its ability to understand and design to the needs of a given customer base and for the exceptional quality of its design work and master planning. For decades, the firm has focused their efforts on the 'customer' and have a unique ability to express their various lifestyles in a compelling strategy.

SUTTLE MINDLIN's work is visually compelling, evocative and emotionally satisfying. And, every one of the firm's commercial developments have succeeded financially because they help create the business strategy or merchandising concepts that are the foundation of their clients' success. The firm has particular expertise in retail, hospitality, healthcare, office buildings, mixed-use, corporate architecture, business interiors, and residential. The practice is founded on repeat business with clients who value the firm's integrity and personal care.

The firm's work spans a wide range of projects that gives SUTTLE MINDLIN a unique vantage point from which to understand culture, lifestyle and the complicated details of their clients' needs. Current projects include master planning 300 acres of 'new urbanism' complete with commercial town center and 1,200 single family homes; corporate office interiors; shopping mall renovations; a new prototype concept for education-based retailing; a revolutionary new concept for the delivery of healthcare in America; country club/hospitality; convention centers, and an entertainment experience called 'The Show About Cars'.

## Swanke Hayden Connell Architects
### New York, New York

Swank Hayden Connell Architects (SHCA) is the continuation of a architectural practice founded in New York in 1906 as Walker & Gillette. Over the years the firm has grown to approximately 250 professionals located in six offices: New York City; Washington DC; Miami, Florida; Stamford, Connecticut; London, and Istanbul.

The firm concentrates on four areas of practice: architecture, interior design, strategic planning, and historic preservation and restoration.

SHCA was founded on two fundamental principles: first, knowing their clients, and their requirements, and second, providing their comprehensive design service in a manner which results in a satisfied client and a successful project.

Their project delivery is the natural outgrowth of these principals. The firm is organized on a team basis and nearly all SHCA professionals work in every area of their practice. This lets them respond to project requirements from a broad base of experience within a single team, allowing the firm to explore with their client the best solutions for new building design, interior design, and methods for renovation and restoration. SHCA is proud of this aspect of their organization for it distinguishes them from others in the field, and has been a vital element contributing to their international success.

## Yabu Pushelburg
### Toronto, Ontario, Canada

Established in 1980 by George Yabu and Glenn Pushelberg, the firm's Creative Director and Managing Partner respectively, Yabu Pushelberg has long built its reputation on providing a myriad of design and marketing solutions for an eclectic and demanding clientele. A distinctly creative enterprise that views its mission to be one of bringing forth creative strategies for business, Yabu Pushelberg develops content right along side its clients, rather than simply giving form to their ideas. Concepts are custom-developed to suit the client's objectives to ensure successful commerce.

A process and deadline-oriented firm, the Yabu Pushelberg approach to design belies the quick fix, cure-all remedy prevalent in most creative practice todayand instead creates timeless signature work. Since 1992, the firm has been engaged in creating a range of furnishings and carpets manufactured and marketed under licensing agreements with ICF/Nienkämper.

With an in-house staff of over 55, including design, technical, and management personnel, the YP team is able to provide each client with a full scope of design and project administration services. Other creative/design facets of the firm include marketing & communications creative, graphic design services, and visual merchandising concepts.

With respect to clients old and new, Yabu Pushelberg has had the great fortune to work with some of the best and most successful businesses in the world in a wide variety of industries.

The firm continues to work out of its 11, 000 sq. ft. offices in Toronto and will soon open a satellite studio in New York.

**Index**

# Acknowledgments

IMAGES is pleased to add "Interior Spaces of the USA and Canada, Volume 5" to its compendium of design and architectural publications.

We wish to thank all participating firms for their valuable contribution to this publication.